The **Diabetes** Update

Alvin and Virginia Silverstein and Laura Silverstein Nunn

Titles in the DISEASE UPDATE series:

DISEASE
UPDATE

The **Diabetes** Update

Alvin and Virginia Silverstein and Laura Silverstein Nunn

Enslow Publishers, Inc.

40 Industrial Road   PO Box 38
Box 398   Aldershot
Berkeley Heights, NJ 07922 Hants GU12 6BP
USA   UK

http://www.enslow.com

Acknowledgment

The authors thank Dr. Anne Marie Van Hoven, a specialist in endocrinology, for her careful reading of the manuscript and her many helpful comments and suggestions.

Library of Congress Cataloging-in-Publication Data

Silverstein, Alvin.
    The diabetes update / Alvin and Virginia Silverstein
and Laura Silverstein Nunn.— 1st ed.
       p. cm. — (Disease update)
    Includes bibliographical references and index.
    ISBN 0-7660-2483-0 (hardcover)
    1. Diabetes—Juvenile literature. I. Silverstein, Virginia B.
II. Nunn, Laura Silverstein. III. Title. IV. Series.
RC660.5.S553 2005
616.4'62—dc22

                        2005005991

Printed in the United States of America

10 9 8 7 6 5 4 3 2 1

To Our Readers: We have done our best to make sure all Internet Addresses in this book were active and appropriate when we went to press. However, the author and the publisher have no control over and assume no liability for the material available on those Internet sites or on other Web sites they may link to. Any comments or suggestions can be sent by e-mail to comments@enslow.com or to the address on the back cover.

Contents

Diabetes

What is it?
A disease in which the body cannot store and use sugar properly, resulting in abnormally high amounts of sugar in the blood.

Who gets it?
Both sexes; all ages (type 1 mainly in children, teenagers, and young adults; type 2 mainly in the middle-aged and elderly, but increasing numbers of younger people are being affected); all races (but more common among African Americans, Native Americans, and Latinos).

How do you get it?
Causes of type 1 diabetes are generally not known, but it may be brought on by certain viral infections; type 2 diabetes may be partly hereditary and may be brought on by obesity.

What are the symptoms?
Unquenchable thirst, frequent need to urinate, weight loss, increased hunger, fatigue, irritability, itchy skin, and poor healing. Uncontrolled diabetes can lead to complications including blindness, nerve damage, kidney disease, and heart disease.

How is it treated?
Diet and exercise; insulin injections for type 1; oral medications or insulin for type 2; islet cell transplants (experimental) and pancreas transplants for type 1.

How can it be prevented?
Diet and exercise can help prevent type 2 diabetes; people at risk can take medications that may prevent the development of the disease.

Professional basketball player Chris Dudley, shown here attempting to block a shot by Alonzo Mourning, was diagnosed with diabetes when he was sixteen years old.

1

The Sugar
Disease

WHEN PROFESSIONAL BASKETBALL player
Chris Dudley was a kid, all he wanted to do
was play basketball. In high school, Chris
worked hard for a spot on the school basketball team.
He was a great athlete and focused all his attention on
his favorite sport. But at sixteen years old, Chris had
something else to focus on—diabetes. "I had all the
classic symptoms: excessive thirst, frequent urination,
always tired," he recalls. "Fortunately my dad's brother,
who also had diabetes, recognized the signs."[1] When the
test results came back, Chris's blood sugar level was over
400 mg/dl. (A normal blood sugar level is less than 100
mg/dl.)

What Is Blood Sugar?

The food we eat is digested (broken down) into simpler chemicals, small enough to pass into the bloodstream. Carbohydrates, such as table sugar and the starch in bread and potatoes, are broken down into simple sugars, mainly one called glucose. Glucose is the body's main fuel. It is carried in the blood to all the body cells, which use it to produce energy for their activities. The blood sugar level is the amount of glucose in the blood, expressed in milligrams per deciliter, or mg/dl. (A deciliter is a tenth of a liter.)

When Chris was told he had diabetes, at first he worried that he would not be able to play basketball again. His doctor assured him that he could still play. But he had to watch his diet and blood sugar. As soon as he heard that, he thought, "I can handle this."[2]

Chris was careful about what he ate. He also checked his blood sugar level regularly, as many as ten times a day. If it was too low, he would eat a snack or drink some fruit juice. If it was too high, he would give himself an insulin shot. (Insulin is a hormone produced in the body that helps the body use sugar properly.) Every day, Chris followed a strict routine to keep his diabetes under control.

Meanwhile, Chris never lost sight of his dream of becoming a basketball star in the NBA. Even though he was not selected by college basketball recruiters, Chris attended Yale University. He became a valuable player on the college basketball team. Then in 1987, at age 22, Chris got his big break into pro basketball when he was drafted by the Cleveland Cavaliers. Over the years, he also played on a number of other teams, including the New York Knicks, the New Jersey Nets, and the Portland Trail Blazers. He achieved the "star player" status that he had always dreamed of. And he earned the respect and admiration of his teammates, coaches, and fans.

Throughout his basketball career, Chris was lucky to work with people who were understanding about his diabetes. As a pro basketball player, keeping a routine was not easy. But Chris made it happen. During games, he tested his sugar level every chance he got. He also took insulin shots when needed. Just as before, if his blood sugar got too low, he ate a snack or guzzled some juice.

In September 2003, Chris Dudley retired from the NBA, but his schedule is just as busy as ever. He now spends much of his time working with the foundation he created in 1994. The Dudley Foundation raises awareness of juvenile diabetes, provides educational programs, and gives money for diabetes research.[3] A big

> Diabetes is sometimes called the sugar disease. That is because people with diabetes cannot use the sugar in their blood properly.

part of the foundation is the Chris Dudley Basketball Camp, which is held every summer. It helps kids with diabetes achieve their goals in sports. They also learn how to manage their condition. But most of all, they learn that diabetes cannot stop them from doing whatever they want to do.[4]

Diabetes is sometimes called the sugar disease. That is because people with diabetes cannot use the sugar in their blood properly. The body either produces little or no insulin, or it does not use the insulin effectively. Insulin is a hormone that helps the body get the energy it needs from sugar. Everybody has some sugar in their blood, but too much sugar in the blood can be harmful.

The Chris Dudley Basketball Camp encourages kids with diabetes to reach their goals in sports. The camp is held every summer.

Famous People with Diabetes[5]

Name	Occupation
Arthur Ashe	Tennis player
Halle Berry	Actress
Phoebe Cates	Actress
Paul Cézanne	Painter
Ty Cobb	Baseball player
Thomas Alva Edison	Inventor
Ella Fitzgerald	Singer
Victor Garber	Actor
Jackie Gleason	Comedian
Mikhail Gorbachev	Politician
Ernest Hemingway	Writer
Pope John Paul II	Religious leader
B. B. King	Blues singer
Tommy Lee	Drummer
Bret Michaels	Rock musician
Mary Tyler Moore	Actress
Elvis Presley	Singer
Jackie Robinson	Baseball player
Sharon Stone	Actress
Elizabeth Taylor	Actress
H.G. Wells	Writer
Vanessa Williams	Singer/Actress

Uncontrolled diabetes can lead to serious health problems, including high blood pressure, kidney failure, blindness, nerve damage, and heart disease.

> Worldwide, about 194 million people have diabetes. And the number continues to rise.

Diabetes is a problem all over the world. Worldwide, about 194 million people have diabetes. And the number continues to rise. Health experts believe that by the year 2025, nearly 333 million people around the world will have diabetes.[6] In the United States alone, diabetes affects about 18.2 million people, a third of whom do not even know they have the disease.[7] Diabetes that goes undetected can be very dangerous. Worldwide, more than 3 million people die every year from complications of diabetes.[8]

There is no medical cure for diabetes, but there are ways to keep the condition under control. Medications can prevent the symptoms. Insulin shots can help keep the blood sugar level under control. Exercising regularly and eating healthy foods are also important. Blood sugar level must also be checked regularly. With a good daily routine, a person with diabetes can live a long, healthy life.

Greek physician Aretaeus of Cappadocia first named diabetes.

Diabetes Through the Ages

DIABETES HAS BEEN AROUND for thousands of years. The first descriptions of the disease were recorded as early as 1500 B.C. in the Ebers Papyrus. The Ebers Papyrus is a comprehensive document that was written in Egypt. It contains medical descriptions and treatments of various illnesses and conditions. Ancient Egyptian doctors described diabetes as the passing of too much urine. They suggested that patients change their diet to include wheat grains, grapes, honey, and berries.

Around 400 B.C., Susruta, a doctor in India, wrote that people with this disease produced "honey urine." Sometimes he used an unusual method to diagnose his

siphon

What's in a Name?

The name *diabetes* comes from a Greek word meaning "siphon." A siphon is a U-shaped tube that transfers liquid from one container to another. Ancient Greek doctors noticed that people with diabetes drank large amounts of liquid, and they had to urinate frequently. The fluid seemed to run right through them, as water runs through a siphon.

patients. He poured a patient's urine over an anthill. If ants were attracted to the urine, the patient probably had diabetes. Ancient Indian doctors thought that the sweetness was caused by eating in excess, especially foods that contained rice, flour, and sugar. They suggested a strict diet that did not include these ingredients.

Around A.D. 100, Greek physician Aretaeus of Cappadocia named the disease diabetes. He also gave a detailed description of the disease at the time: "Diabetes is a dreadful affliction, not very frequent among men, being a melting down of the flesh and limbs into urine. . . . Life is short, unpleasant and painful, thirst unquenchable."[1]

Though a number of ancient doctors had theories about diabetes, the cause was a mystery, and no one could treat it effectively. During the Dark Ages (around A.D. 476 to 1000), when civilizations in Europe were crumbling, much of the old knowledge about diabetes was lost.

Rediscovering Diabetes

It was not until the seventeenth century that strong interest in uncovering the mysteries of diabetes returned. In 1674, Thomas Willis, a physician at Oxford University in England, discovered that the urine of patients with diabetes was sweet. He actually tasted it!

In 1776, another English physician, Matthew Dobson, made the next breakthrough. He proved that the sweet taste of diabetic urine was due to sugar. He boiled urine until it evaporated. What was left was a substance that looked, smelled, and tasted just like brown sugar. He also found sugar in the blood of both healthy people and those with diabetes. Dobson realized that the sugar in the urine of people with diabetes actually came from the blood.

Doctors often had to taste their patients' urine to diagnose diabetes. But in 1790, they breathed a sigh of

What Is Sugar?

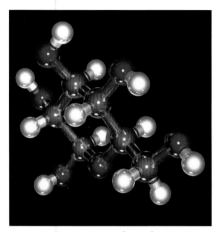
glucose (sugar) molecule

Sugar is not just that white stuff people sprinkle in their coffee or tea. That is only one kind of sugar. Sugars are found in sweet-tasting foods, such as fruits, candy, and ice cream. They belong to a food group called carbohydrates, which are the body's main source of energy. Carbohydrates are made of carbon (blue circle), hydrogen (white), and oxygen (red).

Another type of carbohydrate is starch. Starch is made up of a lot of sugar units linked together. Starchy foods include breads, pasta, and rice.

relief when German physician Johann Peter Frank developed the first new diagnostic test. It was a yeast test that could detect the level of sugar in the urine.

In 1797, British physician John Rollo determined that too much sugar in the blood caused the frequent urination. He then showed that diet played an important role in controlling diabetes. He came up with a diet that was low in carbohydrates and high in fat and protein. He also suggested a steady exercise routine. This treatment of diet and exercise did help some patients, especially those who were overweight. But not much could be done to help children with diabetes. Cutting their diet so severely would not give them enough calories to grow. They usually had only a short time to live.

A popular diabetes diet at the time was even stricter than Rollo's eating plan. Many people went on a "starvation diet." They could have no more than 1,000 calories a day! (An average nine- to eleven-year-old child needs about 2,300 calories a day.) This was supposed to help get rid of the sugar in the urine and help patients live longer. However, many patients lost a lot of weight and became very weak.

The Pancreas Problem

Doctors did not know what caused diabetes. For centuries, it was believed that the frequent urination was caused by a problem with the bladder or the kidneys. In 1788, however, English physician Thomas Cawley discovered a shriveled pancreas when he performed an autopsy on a person with diabetes. (The pancreas is a digestive gland that fits in between the stomach and the small intestine.) He thought that perhaps there was a link between the pancreas and diabetes. But most other scientists did not agree.

What causes diabetes to develop? That question remained a mystery until 1889. Two German scientists, Joseph von Mering and Oskar Minkowski, were trying to prove that the pancreas is involved in the digestion of fats. They removed the pancreas of a dog to see what would happen. After the operation, the dog kept urinating on the laboratory floor. This was strange, since the dog was housebroken and had been taken out regularly. Minkowski realized that frequent urination was a symptom of diabetes. He tested the dog's urine and found it was high in sugar. It appeared that the two researchers had produced diabetes by removing the dog's pancreas. After further studies, they realized that the pancreas releases a substance that affects the way the body uses sugar. But what was it?

In the years that followed, trying to identify that mysterious substance became the focus of a great deal of research. The first step was learning more about the pancreas. This leaf-shaped organ produces digestive enzymes. These chemicals work in the small intestine to break down the proteins, carbohydrates, and fats in foods. Back in 1869, a German biologist named Paul Langerhans had reported that small "islands" (he called them islets) of strange-looking cells are scattered

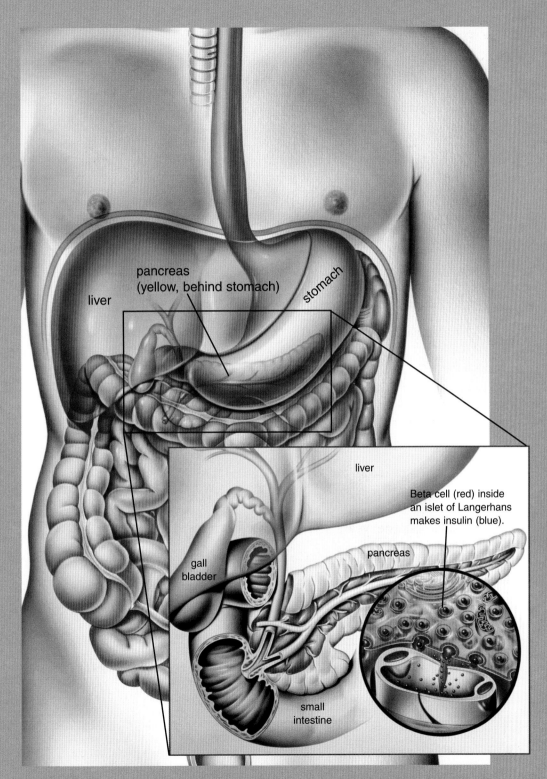

The pancreas is an organ located near the stomach. The islets of Langerhans inside the pancreas make hormones. These hormones help the body use sugar.

through the pancreas. He did not realize the importance of what he had found.

It was not until the early 1900s that researchers realized that the pancreas is actually two organs in one. Laboratory studies showed that if the islets of Langerhans in an animal's pancreas were damaged, symptoms of diabetes developed. But if the rest of the pancreas was damaged while the islets were not, no diabetes symptoms developed. The researchers suggested that the islets do not produce digestive enzymes, like the rest of the pancreas. Instead, they make hormones, proteins that help to control body processes. The islets actually produce hormones that work on the body's use of sugar. The pancreas, then, is both a digestive organ and an endocrine (hormone-producing) organ. For a long time, however, efforts to obtain pure samples of hormones from the pancreas were unsuccessful.

Searching for the Mystery Hormone

In 1920, a Canadian surgeon, Frederick Banting, became intrigued after reading a journal article about diabetes and the search for the mysterious hormone. He started thinking. It seemed that the digestive juices in the pancreas must be destroying the hormone in the

The 1923 Nobel Prize in Medicine went to John J. R. Macleod (left) and Frederick Banting. They shared the prize with colleagues Charles Best and James Bertram Collip.

Dr. Frederick Banting (standing) and Dr. Charles Best in the lab in 1921.

islets of Langerhans before it can be isolated. Banting figured that if he could stop the pancreas from working, but keep the islets of Langerhans going, then maybe he could find the hormone.

Banting went to Professor John J. R. Macleod, the head of the department of physiology at the University of Toronto, to ask for support. It took some convincing, but finally Macleod gave Banting some laboratory space, ten experimental dogs, and a graduate student named Charles Best to help with the experiments.

In May 1921, Banting and Best removed the pancreases of several healthy dogs. From these organs they extracted (removed) material from the islets of Langerhans and injected it into the dogs (which had become diabetic after the surgery). The dogs' abnormally high blood sugar levels quickly dropped. In fact, if enough of the extract was injected, the blood sugar level dropped below normal. However, there were some problems purifying the extract. Macleod brought in another researcher, James Bertram Collip, to help out. Within about six weeks, the researchers had a purified extract they believed was ready for human use. They named it insulin.

In January 1922, a fourteen-year-old boy named

Leonard Thompson became the first person to receive an insulin injection. Leonard had been diagnosed with diabetes two years earlier. Doctors had given him the only treatment they knew of—a starvation diet of only 450 calories a day. He weighed only sixty-five pounds, and he was dying. The first insulin injection did not go very well. Leonard's arm became red and swollen. His blood sugar level decreased, but not by much. The

In January 1922, a fourteen-year-old boy named Leonard Thompson became the first person to receive an insulin injection.

researchers went back to the lab and worked hard to make the serum less toxic. About two weeks later, Leonard was given a second injection of insulin. This time it worked! His blood sugar level came down dramatically. His symptoms started to disappear, and he was beginning to feel normal again. The insulin injections allowed Leonard to control his diabetes. News about the success of insulin spread around the world like wildfire.

LEONARD THOMPSON
First patient to receive insulin in Toronto.

Fourteen-year-old Leonard Thompson was the first patient to receive an insulin injection. This successful treatment controlled his diabetes.

The following year, insulin became widely available to people with diabetes all over the world. It was produced from pancreases taken from cattle and pigs used for meat. That same year, 1923, a Nobel Prize in Medicine was awarded to Banting and Macleod for the insulin breakthrough. Banting was very upset that his partner, Charles Best, was not acknowledged for all his work on the discovery. At first, he refused to accept the award. Eventually he did, but he gave half of his

In 1923, insulin became widely available to people with diabetes all over the world.

share of the award money to Best. Likewise, Macleod gave half of his award money to Collip.[2]

Insulin was undoubtedly a landmark discovery. For Leonard Thompson and countless others, insulin allowed them to survive. At the time, it seemed as if insulin was the answer. As a result, research to cure diabetes stopped. Instead, medical experts spent more time trying to figure out how to control the disease

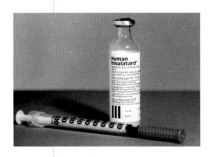

What's the Difference?

For more than half a century, pork and beef insulin helped people with diabetes to survive. These animal insulins are so similar to the human hormone that people can take them without any serious problems. But chemically they are not *exactly* the same. Researchers believed that human insulin would probably work even better, but not much was available. Small amounts, mainly for research studies, were taken from the bodies of people who died. In 1983, scientists succeeded in genetically engineering bacteria to make human insulin. The bacteria could be grown in huge tanks, producing the large amounts needed to meet the needs of people with diabetes. Studies showed that in most cases this human insulin controlled the blood sugar level better and produced fewer side effects than animal insulins.

better and how to live with it. However, about a decade after the insulin discovery, people were becoming unhappy with long-term insulin therapy. Some people did not want to deal with daily injections. Others were too old or weak to do so. It was also tough getting the dose of insulin just right. Taking too much or too little could be dangerous. Furthermore, the majority of diabetes cases are not caused by a simple lack of insulin.

The disease is much more complicated than doctors had realized. Researchers started to look for better ways to treat diabetes.

Exploring Alternative Treatments

In 1966, Dr. Richard Lillehei and Dr. William Kelly performed the first pancreas transplant on a twenty-eight-year-old woman. At first it seemed to be a success. The insulin injections were stopped, and the transplanted pancreas (obtained from a person who had died) took over and supplied the hormone the patient needed. But the new pancreas stopped working after about two months. The woman's body had identified the organ as foreign and rejected it. She died a month later, from complications of the surgery. It was clear that developing successful methods for pancreas transplants was going to be a long, difficult task.

By 1978, surgeons were ready to try again. This time, the patient managed to stay off insulin for seventeen years. She died after being thrown off her horse—not from the surgical procedure she had had years before.

Researchers continued to improve surgical techniques and drugs to prevent the body from rejecting the transplant (attacking and destroying it).

By transplanting only the "tail" of the pancreas, they were able to use living donors in some cases. (Rejection problems are greatly reduced when the donor is closely related to the patient.) The two halves of the pancreas were able to produce enough insulin to keep both the donor and the transplant patient healthy. Later, researchers found that it was not necessary to transplant the entire pancreas—just the insulin-producing cells were enough to do the job. In recent years, this has been one main focus of diabetes research.

Another major research effort has been to develop drugs to control blood sugar level. As scientists have learned more about how the insulin system works, they have developed more effective drugs for treating diabetes. Some of these drugs help the body make more insulin. Others help the body use insulin more effectively.

3

What Is Diabetes?

MARC BOLLINGER was in his senior year at Texas Tech University. Soon he would be graduating. He already had a job interview lined up. His life was all planned out. But something happened that changed Marc's plans.

Shortly after the New Year in 2003, Marc started craving soft drinks. He often drank five to six cans a day. He also started eating lots and lots of fast food. Marc could not understand why he seemed to be thirsty all the time. Every morning when he woke up, his mouth was extremely dry. He had to drink about 12 ounces of apple juice to try to quench his thirst. As the days went by, Marc noticed that he had to have a drink with him

Marc Bollinger was diagnosed with diabetes during his senior year of college.
He celebrated his wedding to Jodi a year later.

wherever he went. Since it was wintertime, he just figured he was really thirsty because the air was so dry.

Around mid-February, Marc noticed that he was losing weight. His belly no longer hung over his belt. The new exercise routine he had recently started with his fiancée, Jodi, must be working, he thought.

On February 24, Marc started getting dizzy while he was working at his computer. It got so bad, he could hardly focus on the monitor. He called Jodi and asked her to come over. Marc was in pretty bad shape, so Jodi took him to the health center on campus. Now he was feeling nauseous, too. The nurse checked Marc's height, weight, and blood pressure. Marc could not believe the scale reading when he saw it. It was 120. How could that be? He had weighed 145 pounds just two months before. The doctor asked Marc about his symptoms. He told him he was feeling nauseous and dizzy, and he had a slight headache. The doctor told Marc that he had a sinus infection. He told him to take over-the-counter medicine and get some rest.

A week later, Marc was not getting better. In fact, he felt worse. His vision was getting really bad. He could hardly focus on anything anymore. His headaches were getting more severe. He also felt sick to his stomach most of the time.

Jodi drove Marc to the emergency room. There the doctor told him what the previous doctor had said, that he had a sinus infection. He prescribed antibiotics and sent Marc home.

Over the next couple of days, Marc's symptoms continued to get worse. By this time, he was drinking two large bottles of apple juice within a twelve-hour period. He was also going to the bathroom almost every hour. Marc was really frustrated. He decided to call his dad, who is a doctor, to ask his advice. Marc's father asked him some questions. "Have you noticed that you've lost weight recently?" Marc replied that he had lost 25 pounds in the past few months. Then his dad quickly asked, "Have you been urinating a lot and drinking heavy amounts of fluids?" Marc told him that he had. Right away his dad knew: "You have diabetes." He told Marc to come home right away.

At home, Marc had blood tests done at the hospital in Temple, Texas, where his dad worked. The test results showed a blood glucose level of 383 mg/dl. That was nearly four times the normal level. His body was not making enough insulin. That meant that he was going to need daily insulin shots. At the hospital, they showed Marc how to inject insulin himself and how to test his blood sugar.

Marc took his condition seriously. He started watching what he ate. He gave himself insulin shots every day. He also checked his blood sugar level regularly. He just wanted to feel normal again.

Today, Marc does have control over his diabetes. He has a daily routine that he can live with. Diabetes did not stop Marc from making it to his job interview, or living a normal life.[1]

What's Wrong with Sugar?

For most people, sugar is just a normal part of life. It is in most of the food we eat every day, especially in cookies, cakes, and ice cream. Of course, too much of it is not good for anybody. But in people with diabetes, sugar can become dangerous.

When doctors talk about diabetes, they use its full name, diabetes mellitus. *Mellitus* is Latin for "honey-sweet." People with diabetes mellitus have sugar in their urine. This name helps to distinguish it from a much rarer form of the disease, called diabetes insipidus, or "bland diabetes." People with that type also produce

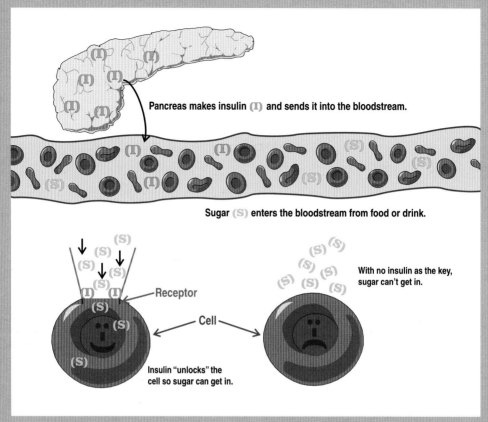

Pancreas makes insulin (I) and sends it into the bloodstream.

Sugar (S) enters the bloodstream from food or drink.

Receptor

Cell

Insulin "unlocks" the cell so sugar can get in.

With no insulin as the key, sugar can't get in.

Insulin is the "key" that lets sugar into the cell. Then the cell uses the sugar for energy.

large amounts of urine, but the urine does not contain sugar.

Diabetes mellitus is a disease that results in high levels of sugar in the blood. Having some sugar in the blood is normal. In fact, it is essential. Much of the food we eat is turned into a sugar called glucose. Some of the glucose is stored, and some of it is used right away, for energy. Glucose provides the energy that makes the brain work, the heart pump, and the muscles move. It is also needed to nourish all of the cells and tissues in the body.

Carbohydrates are a good source of glucose. They give the body the energy it needs. Through digestion, food is broken down so that glucose can be absorbed into the bloodstream. The glucose is carried through a network of blood vessels to various parts of the body, where the glucose is used as energy. The pancreas, an organ that lies near the stomach, makes a hormone called insulin. Insulin's main job is to get the glucose from the bloodstream into the body's cells. You can think of insulin as a "key" that glucose uses to "unlock the doors" to the cells. Without this important key, the body cells do not get the glucose they need for fuel.

> Insulin's main job is to get the glucose from the bloodstream into the body's cells. You can think of insulin as a "key" that glucose uses to "unlock the doors" to the cells.

Insulin also works in other ways to lower the amount of sugar in the blood. It helps liver and muscle cells change glucose into a starch. This starch is stored in the liver and provides a source of sugar for the body's energy needs between meals. Insulin also helps fat cells change glucose into fatty acids, another form of energy

Balancing Act

Insulin helps control the amount of sugar in the blood. When the amount of sugar in the blood rises, the pancreas releases insulin. Insulin makes the blood sugar level go down by helping the sugar in the blood pass into the body cells. But insulin does not work alone. When the blood sugar level falls, the pancreas releases another hormone, called glucagon. Glucagon makes the blood sugar level go up by causing starch (stored in the body cells) to turn into glucose. The glucose then goes into the blood and is carried to the cells that need energy.

Insulin and glucagon work together as a team to balance each other out. They make sure that the amount of sugar in the blood is always just right. When diabetes develops, this balancing act falls apart.

storage. When insulin is not working properly, extra sugar builds up in the blood. As a result, symptoms of diabetes develop.

Types of Diabetes

There are two main types of diabetes mellitus: type 1 and type 2. Type 1 diabetes used to be called juvenile diabetes. That is because it is often first noticed in children, teenagers, and young adults. However, it can occur at any age if the pancreas no longer produces insulin, or if it does not produce enough of it. Type 1 diabetes can appear suddenly. A person can feel fine one day and then very sick the next. Type 1 diabetes can be very dangerous. It is very important to correct blood sugar level with daily insulin injections. Otherwise, dangerous complications may develop.

Why does the pancreas stop producing insulin? Type 1 diabetes develops because the body's own immune system destroys beta cells. Beta cells are the cells of the pancreas that produce insulin. The immune system is the body's defense system. It contains a powerful team of defenders, the white blood cells. These white blood cells are supposed to protect the body against invading bacteria or viruses. However, the body's defenders may mistake beta cells for intruders—and then destroy them. (This kind of mistaken attack on the body's own cells is called an autoimmune reaction.) Diabetes develops when at least 90 percent of the pancreatic beta cells have been destroyed.[2] Type 1 diabetes, however, accounts for only 5 to 10 percent of all diabetes cases.[3]

There are two main types of diabetes mellitus: type 1 and type 2. Type 2 diabetes is the most common form. It accounts for about 90 to 95 percent of all diabetes cases.

Is It Type 1 or Type 2?

Type 1 Diabetes	Type 2 Diabetes
5 to 10 percent of all diabetes cases	90 to 95 percent of all diabetes cases
Appears at younger ages	Appears at older ages
Starts suddenly	Develops gradually
No insulin or very little is produced	Some insulin is produced, but it does not work properly
Blood sugar is above normal	Blood sugar is above normal
Extreme weight loss is typical	Obesity is common
Extreme thirst	Extreme thirst
Frequent urination	Frequent urination
Feeling weak and tired	Feeling weak and tired
Sores, slow healing, blurred vision, leg pains	Sores, slow healing, blurred vision, leg pains

Type 2 diabetes is the most common form. It accounts for about 90 to 95 percent of all diabetes cases.[4] It affects mostly adults who are over forty years old. However, more and more young people, including children, are developing this type.

In the early stages of type 2 diabetes, the pancreas *does* produce insulin. However, the body cannot use it properly. For some reason, the body's cells do not respond to insulin. Doctors call this condition insulin resistance, or prediabetes. More than 60 million Americans have insulin resistance, but only 25 percent of those with insulin resistance will develop type 2 diabetes.[5] Prediabetes does not mean a person has diabetes, just that the blood sugar level is somewhat higher than normal. It indicates an increased risk for developing type 2 diabetes.

How does prediabetes turn into type 2 diabetes? When the blood sugar level starts to rise, the need for insulin becomes greater. The pancreas releases more and more insulin to try to get the sugar level normal. Eventually, the beta cells in the pancreas wear out and can no longer make enough insulin. As a result, sugar builds up in the blood. Type 2 diabetes can take years to develop.

What's Normal?

According to the American Diabetes Association:

Normal	=	blood sugar level less than 100 mg/dl
Prediabetes	=	blood sugar level between 100 and 125 mg/dl
Diabetes	=	blood sugar level above 125 mg/dl

What Are the Symptoms?

You may wonder how Marc's doctors—both of them—could have misdiagnosed his condition. Part of the problem was probably the fact that Marc did not recognize the key symptoms of diabetes—extreme thirst, frequent urination, and unexplained weight loss. At the time, it seemed to make sense that he was thirsty all the time because the climate was so dry. And of course, anyone who drinks a lot of liquids will have to go to the bathroom a lot. He wondered about his loss of weight but did not connect it with his illness. When the doctors asked about Marc's symptoms, he did not think

Temporary Diabetes

People who have diabetes have to live with it for the rest of their lives. Some pregnant women, however, develop a type of diabetes that disappears after the baby is born. This condition is called gestational diabetes. (*Gestation* is another word for pregnancy.) Women who develop gestational diabetes have a greater risk for problems during pregnancy. After the pregnancy, as many as 50 percent of those who had gestational diabetes may develop type 2 diabetes later in life.[6]

Symptom Checklist

Here are some warning signs of type 1 and type 2 diabetes. People with diabetes may:

- be thirsty all the time
- have to urinate frequently
- feel weak and tired
- feel hungry all the time
- lose weight, even though they eat a lot
- get sores on their skin that take a long time to heal
- notice that objects look fuzzy or blurry
- have pain, tingling, or numbness in their fingers, legs, or feet

Anybody can have some of these warning signs from time to time without having diabetes. However, people who have many of these signs, and have them all the time, should see a doctor.

to mention those that were most characteristic of the disease. Fortunately, Marc's dad was able to ask the questions that would finally lead to an accurate diagnosis.

When the blood sugar level is very high, some of the excess sugar in the blood gets into the urine. How does that happen? Urine is made in the kidneys. The kidneys take out waste products from the blood. They also take

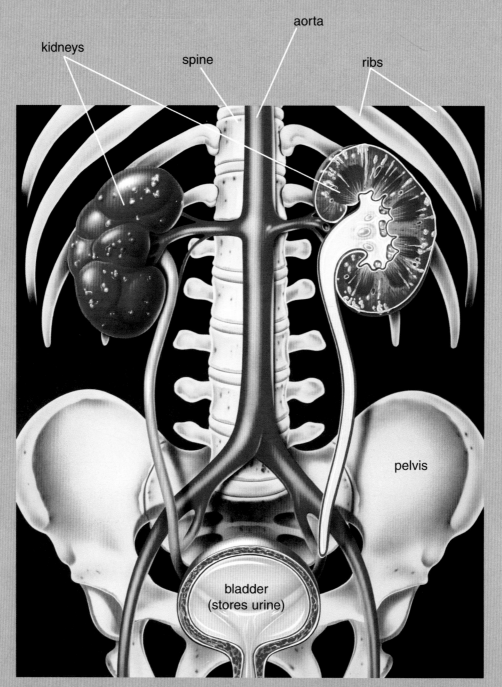

kidneys

aorta

spine

ribs

pelvis

bladder
(stores urine)

When a person has diabetes, the kidneys have to work extra hard. This causes more frequent urination and greater thirst.

out some water to flush the wastes away. If there is too much of something in the blood, the kidneys take that out too. People with diabetes have too much sugar in their blood, and soon sugar winds up in their urine.

When sugar passes into urine, it brings more water with it. This extra water washes out other things, too. Vitamins, minerals, proteins, and fats are lost along with the sugar and water. That is why the warning signs develop. If you have diabetes, for example, the kidneys make a lot of urine because they are getting rid of the

What's That Smell?

The breath of people with uncontrolled diabetes often has a fruity smell. This is caused by ketones. Ketones are chemicals that are formed when fat is burned for energy. These chemicals build up in the blood and pass into the urine.

Too many ketones can poison or even kill body cells. If the body has to burn off a lot of fat because there is not enough insulin available to use the sugar, a condition called ketoacidosis develops. When this happens, headaches, tiredness, confusion, dry mouth, stomach pain, and breathing problems may develop. The person may lose consciousness and go into a diabetic coma and—if not given prompt medical attention—may die. Ketoacidosis may develop in people with type 1 diabetes. It rarely occurs in people with type 2 diabetes.

extra sugar from the blood. So you have to make a lot of trips to the bathroom. You are also thirsty all the time because you are losing so much water. You feel unusually weak and tired because your body cannot use sugar for the energy it needs. You are hungry because you are losing many other good food materials, which are also getting washed out in your urine.

Complications of Diabetes

Uncontrolled diabetes can lead to a number of other health problems. These complications may include the following:

Blood vessel damage: Diabetes causes blood vessels to narrow and harden. This can lead to a heart attack or stroke. A heart attack happens when the heart's blood supply is cut off by a blood clot blocking an artery leading to the heart. A stroke happens when the blood supply to a part of the brain is cut off. Adults with diabetes are two to four times more likely to have a heart attack or a stroke than people without diabetes.[7]

Infections: People with diabetes have a greater risk of getting sick. High blood sugar weakens the immune system. Germs can use sugar to grow and multiply quickly.

Eye damage: People with diabetes have a greater risk of developing eye problems. In most cases, the damage is minor. However, the problems can become more serious and result in blindness. This happens when the high sugar content in the blood damages the blood vessels that nourish the eyes. Diabetes is the number one cause of blindness in middle-aged people in the United States.

Kidney damage: The kidneys are hardworking organs. Inside them are millions of blood vessels that filter 50 gallons of fluid from the blood every day. Kidney problems develop when damage to the blood vessels causes problems in their filtering system.

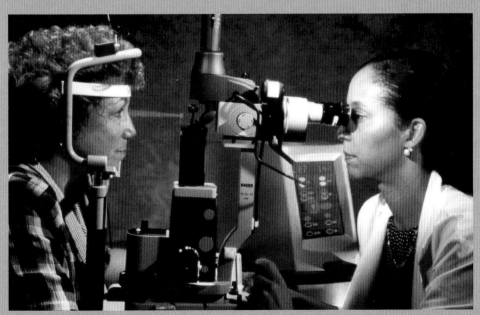

This diabetes patient has an eye disease, which is being treated with a laser.

Nerve damage: Damage to the nerves may result in a loss of feeling in the hands and feet. This can be especially dangerous because some people may not realize when they have injured their foot. Without immediate medical attention, an infection may develop.

Foot problems: Poor circulation (blood flow) is a big problem in people with diabetes. Diabetes causes blood vessels in the foot to become narrow and hard. Blood contains nutrients and other substances that cells need for growth and repair. With less blood reaching the feet, infections may take a long time to heal. Problems in healing, together with nerve damage to the foot, may result in the need for amputation (surgical removal of a limb).

4

What Causes Diabetes?

In 2003, Hillary Carroll spent Memorial Day at her grandmother's house. It was an unusually warm day, and the swimming pool had just opened up. Hillary could not wait to enjoy her first swim of the season. She had a lot of fun swimming all day long. By nighttime, though, Hillary did not feel right. Every time she went to the bathroom, she doubled over in pain. Her mother thought that she might have a urinary tract infection. Hillary's mother immediately drove her to the hospital, where they ran some tests. The lab results showed that Hillary did not have an infection—she had type 2 diabetes.

How could Hillary have type 2 diabetes? Her mother could not believe it. Type 2 diabetes usually strikes adults. Hillary was only ten years old—but she weighed 220 pounds. Generally, type 2 diabetes is thought to be a problem that affects people over forty. In fact, it used to be called adult-onset diabetes. That name was changed because more and more young people were getting this type of diabetes. Why has this type begun to affect so many kids? Part of the reason is that obesity (being seriously overweight) is a growing problem in the United States. And obesity is a big factor in developing type 2 diabetes.[1]

After Hillary was diagnosed, she had to stay in the hospital for a week to get her blood sugar level normal.

> Obesity (being seriously overweight) is a growing problem in the United States. And obesity is a big factor in developing type 2 diabetes.

When she got out of the hospital, she had to have two insulin shots and swallow two pills every day. After two years, Hillary was able to control her diabetes through diet, exercise, and four pills a day. She was also working on losing weight. Just six months after her diagnosis, Hillary had lost thirty-five pounds.[2]

Watch What You Eat

A common myth about diabetes is that people can get it by eating too many sweets. That is not exactly true. Eating sweets cannot *cause* diabetes, but eating too many of them—or too much of anything—can lead to weight gain. Being overweight increases the risk for developing type 2 diabetes. So watch what you eat!

A Weight Problem

One of the biggest factors in developing type 2 diabetes is being overweight. Although there are some thin people with type 2 diabetes, nearly 90 percent are overweight.[3] People become overweight when they eat more food than the body needs to fuel its activities. Too much of any food can cause a weight problem. What the body does not use, it stores as fat. People who are extremely overweight are called obese.

How can obesity lead to diabetes? When a person eats a heavy meal, the blood sugar level rises. This signals the body to produce insulin. If the person is likely to develop diabetes, insulin resistance may make the body cells unable to use insulin effectively. The increased demands for insulin during years of overeating may overwork the beta cells. After a while, these insulin-making cells may get worn out or damaged. Medical researchers have found that about half of the beta cells are no longer working by the time type 2 diabetes is diagnosed.[4]

Health experts say that more children are getting diabetes than ever before. "If you go back 20 years, about 2 percent of all cases of new onset diabetes (type 2) were in people between 9 and 19 years old. Now, it's about 30 percent to 50 percent," Dr. Gerald Bernstein, a former president of the American Diabetes Association, remarked in 2004.[5] This increase is probably because many kids today are eating too much food that is high

> Health experts say that more children are getting diabetes than ever before.

in fat and sugar. They also do not get enough exercise. Instead, many of them spend much of their time in front of the television or using the computer. Millions

Students at Rogers Middle School in San Antonio, Texas, exercise on some equipment that is used in a program to reduce the risk of type 2 diabetes. Poor diet and lack of exercise are leading causes of type 2 diabetes in young people.

of children in the United States are obese. As long as obesity continues to be a problem in this country, we can probably expect the risk for type 2 diabetes to increase as well. However, there is no link between obesity and type 1 diabetes.

Are Genes to Blame?

Scientists believe that a person has an increased risk of developing diabetes if someone in his or her family has it. Studies have shown that diabetes can be inherited when certain genes are passed from one generation to the next. Genes are chemicals that carry "blueprints"— a kind of book of instructions—that determine a person's traits, such as curly hair, brown eyes, or big feet. Biologists believe the genes that make it more likely for someone to develop type 2 diabetes are involved in how the body uses food for energy. Groups that have unusually high diabetes rates, such as Pima Indians and African Americans, have a history of times of starvation. People who could get along on less food

Tale of Twin Studies

Scientists were able to show a link between genes and diabetes by studying sets of identical twins—siblings who share the exact same genes. They discovered that heredity plays a more important role in type 2 diabetes than in type 1. For example, if one identical twin has type 1 diabetes, then the other twin has a 35 percent chance of developing the disease. But if one twin has type 2 diabetes, then the other twin as an 80 to 100 percent chance of developing the disease.[6]

were more likely to survive starvation. They passed their genes on to their children. In the United States today, where fast food is cheap and plentiful, those same genes cause the extra food to be stored as fat. This weight gain can lead to insulin resistance and diabetes.[7]

Even if someone in your family has diabetes, that does not necessarily mean you will get it. Health experts say that environmental factors, such as weight gain, combined with the effects of genes, can lead to the development of type 2 diabetes. Studies have shown that certain viruses may be involved in the development of type 1 diabetes. In 2003, researchers found that fourteen different viruses, including Coxsackie B virus, rubella virus, and Epstein-Barr virus, can damage beta cells.[8] In general, it does not seem that a single factor causes diabetes. People cannot change their genes, but they can do things to decrease the effects of the environment, such as getting plenty of exercise and eating healthy foods, but not overeating.

Who Is At Risk?

Anyone can develop diabetes, but certain factors can increase a person's risk or likelihood of developing the disease. As mentioned earlier, diabetes is not caused by a single factor, but by a combination of factors. Risk factors are not as obvious in type 1 diabetes as they are in type 2. The following list includes known risk factors for type 2 diabetes:

- Family history of diabetes
- Being overweight or obese
- Age: being over forty years old
- Lacking physical activity
- Having prediabetes
- History of diabetes during pregnancy
- Belonging to a minority group: Compared to American whites of the same age, African Americans are about 60 percent more likely and Native Americans are more than twice as likely to have diabetes. Hispanics and Latino Americans are about 50 percent more likely to have diabetes than non-Hispanic whites of the same age. Some groups of Asian Americans and Pacific Islanders also have an increased risk.[9]

5

Testing and Treatment

JULIA BUZBY WAS FOURTEEN years old when she found out she had type 1 diabetes. She nearly lost her life before anybody discovered she had the disease. It happened in 1996, when Julia suddenly collapsed. She was rushed to the hospital and was close to a diabetic coma. Luckily, the doctors were able to save her.

Julia had to stay in the hospital for a week before she was well enough to go home. Thinking back, her mother recalls that her daughter's breath had had a fruity smell, a telltale sign of the disease. She did not think anything of it at the time. Julia had shown some other signs, as well. For example, she was drinking up to a gallon of milk a day, she was tired all the time, and she was losing weight. The Buzby family did not know much about diabetes or what to look for. "If we would have known, we would have gotten her to a doctor quicker," remarked Mrs. Buzby.[1]

Julia knows how lucky she is to be alive. After the diagnosis, she and her family tried to learn everything they could about diabetes. Since her body was no longer making enough insulin, she had to learn how to give herself daily insulin shots. Later, she discovered a better way to get her daily supply of insulin instead of injections. She now wears an insulin pump, a device that sends a continual supply of the hormone into her blood. The device looks like a pager and attaches to her belt. The other end is a thin tube that inserts under her skin and gives her the insulin. With the insulin pump, Julia has been able to live a normal, active life. In high school, she became involved in a number of clubs and even tried out for the tennis team.[2]

Millions of people are diagnosed with diabetes every year, and yet, millions of others go undiagnosed. Many people have heard about diabetes, but they may not know what it is or what to look for. Signs and symptoms are usually characteristic of the disease—unusual thirst,

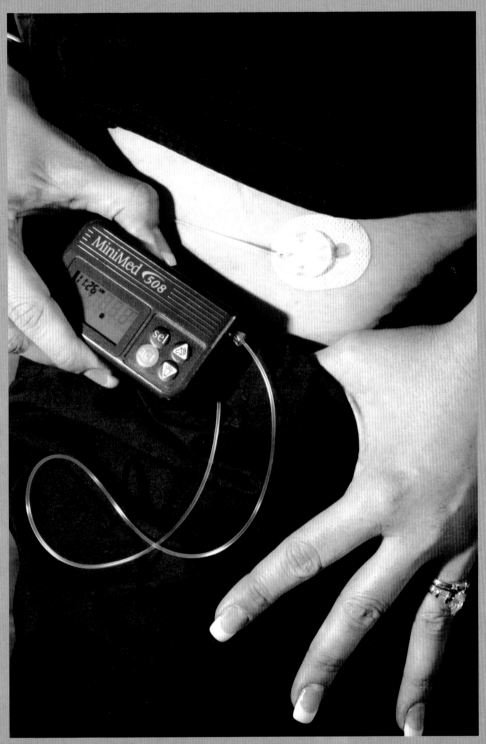

An insulin pump looks like a small pager. It pumps insulin into the body throughout the day.

Blood Is Better

In the past, urine tests were used to detect diabetes. Now doctors depend more on blood tests. Urine tests do not do a good job of showing the blood glucose level. Glucose does not pass into the urine until there is already quite a lot of glucose in the blood.

frequent urination, fatigue, and sudden, unexplained weight loss. Anybody who is having some of these symptoms should see a doctor as soon as possible. If diabetes is suspected, there are a number of tests that can give a positive diagnosis.

Testing for Glucose

The easiest way to detect diabetes is to do a plasma glucose test. This test measures how much glucose is in the blood. Blood can be taken with a needle in your arm or even with a little finger prick. Only a small amount of blood is needed.

Although a glucose test can be done at any time of the day, the results will vary greatly depending on when you last ate. Remember that eating raises the blood sugar level. A fasting plasma glucose test is taken early in the morning, before you have eaten anything. A normal reading after fasting should be less than 100 milligrams of glucose per deciliter of blood. A person with a fasting glucose level between 100 and 125 mg/dl has prediabetes. A person with diabetes will have a fasting glucose level that is more than 125 mg/dl. Two fasting glucose tests taken on different days are needed to make an accurate diagnosis of diabetes.

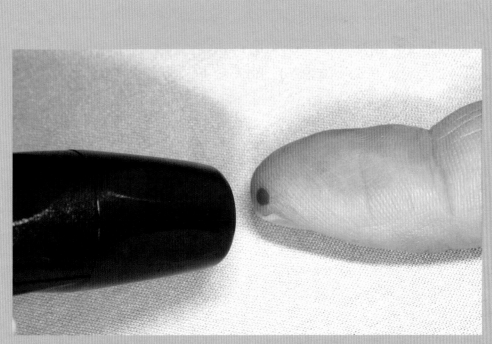

This penlet device is used to take a blood sample for glucose testing.

The glucose tolerance test gives more information on how the body handles sugar. The blood sugar is first tested after fasting. Then a patient drinks a concentrated sugar solution. Blood samples are then taken several times over the next three hours and tested for the amount of glucose. At first, the glucose drink makes the blood sugar level rise, but then the level falls. It is usually back to normal after two to three hours. In people with diabetes, the blood sugar goes up much higher after taking the glucose drink, and it falls more slowly. Even after three hours it may still be high.

A person with diabetes will have a fasting glucose level that is more than 125 mg/dl. Two fasting glucose tests taken on different days are needed to make an accurate diagnosis of diabetes.

Once diabetes is confirmed, treatment should begin right away.

Insulin Treatment

Since diabetes is caused by a lack of working insulin, a common treatment is to put insulin into the body. At the moment, there is no insulin pill you can swallow or liquid that you can drink. Insulin has to be injected into the skin. The needle does not squirt insulin directly

What Should You Do If You Have Diabetes?

Diabetes treatment is very individual. If you have been diagnosed with diabetes, you and your doctor will work out a treatment program that is just right for you. A nutritionist may also have some suggestions. The treatment plan may have to be changed from time to time, if your body's needs change. Generally the plan will include:

- Monitoring (testing) your blood sugar level regularly (see Chapter 6)

- Eating a healthy diet—and not overeating

- Getting active with exercise or sports (your doctor will advise you how active you can be)

- Taking medications to control your blood sugar level if necessary (insulin for type 1 and maybe for type 2 diabetes; oral diabetes drugs for type 2)

A person with diabetes can give himself insulin injections. The insulin helps keep the blood sugar at a healthy level.

into the blood. Instead, it goes into a muscle or fatty area. That way the body can absorb the hormone more slowly rather than all at once. Some common places for injecting insulin are the thighs, buttocks, belly, or upper arms.

People with type 1 diabetes need to have insulin shots several times a day to keep their condition under control. Most people cannot go to the doctor every single day for shots. That is why there are special kits that allow diabetes patients to give insulin shots to themselves. Parents usually give shots to their young children with diabetes. Older kids can learn to give insulin shots to themselves. Kids with diabetes say that it can be pretty scary giving themselves a shot at first.

No More Needles?

An insulin inhaler is being tested on human patients and should be available in the near future. The hormone is breathed into the lungs through a mouthpiece. This is especially good news for people who do not like needles. Health experts say that people with type 1 diabetes may still need injections, but using an insulin inhaler may cut down the number of injections they need.

But after a while, it becomes routine, like getting dressed or brushing their teeth.

> **People with type 1 diabetes need to have insulin shots several times a day to keep their condition under control.**

There are some devices that make taking insulin easier. An automatic injector can shoot the needle into the skin so fast that a person can hardly feel it. Insulin pens are also a popular choice. An insulin pen looks just like a regular ink pen, but instead of a writing tip, it has a needle. Instead of an ink cartridge, it contains an insulin cartridge. Insulin pens are simple to use and can be carried around in a pocket. The needles are very small, and most people find them almost painless to use.

Insulin shots may need to be given several times each day, the way insulin is released from a healthy pancreas. Normally, a person's body makes insulin after eating, which boosts the blood sugar level. Then, as the blood sugar level falls between meals, the pancreas releases less insulin. To keep their blood sugar levels normal, people with diabetes should receive insulin before each meal and again at night, just before bed.

Several different kinds of insulin help control the blood glucose level. Short-acting insulin works quickly and is good for taking before a meal. Long- or medium-acting insulin takes longer to start working but lasts longer. This should be taken before bed. The nighttime injection keeps the glucose level normal during sleep.

Having to take an injection several times a day may seem like a hassle. Instead, many people are using an insulin pump, which can give them doses of the hormone automatically. The cost of these small devices is covered by most insurance programs. A tiny built-in computer works the pump and sends exactly the right amount of insulin into the body. It can also deliver an extra dose just before a meal. A person has to do some experimenting at first to figure out the right amount of insulin flow. However, researchers are working on devices that also test the amount of glucose in the blood and

Many people are using an insulin pump, which can give them doses of insulin automatically. A tiny built-in computer works the pump and sends exactly the right amount of insulin into the body.

adjust the insulin dose automatically—just like a real pancreas.

Diet and Exercise

Many people who have type 2 diabetes do not need daily insulin injections. They may take pills to keep their blood sugar under control. The pills do not contain insulin. Some are drugs that help the body make more insulin. Others lower insulin resistance to make the person's own insulin work better.

Exercise is very important in keeping diabetes under control. The body burns sugar for energy during exercise, causing the blood glucose level to drop. Exercise also burns up food that might otherwise be stored in the body as fat. It helps a person avoid obesity, which can make diabetes symptoms worse.

A healthy diet is also very important. You might think that someone with diabetes should never eat sugar or any sweet foods. That is not exactly true. Everybody needs *some* sugar, but the body can get it from starches and other foods. The problem with eating candy or other high-sugar foods is that much of their sugar does not need to be digested. It goes right into the blood, and the blood glucose level shoots up. Then you

Exercise is an important part of keeping diabetes under control.

need more insulin—fast! Starches and other complex carbohydrates, such as those found in whole-grain bread, pasta, or brown rice, do need to be digested. They provide glucose for the blood slowly and gradually.

A healthy diet for people with diabetes is basically the same as nutritionists recommend for everybody. It includes a wide variety of foods, such as vegetables, whole grains, fruits, low-fat dairy products, beans, nuts, and lean meat, poultry, and fish. People with diabetes

> Eating a healthy diet and getting plenty of exercise
>
> help fight obesity and diabetes.

must watch their portion sizes carefully to avoid eating more than their body needs. (People who are very active physically may need more food than people who are not.) Foods that are high in vitamins, minerals, and fiber are better choices than refined or processed foods such as pastries, donuts, and white bread.

Eating a healthy diet and getting plenty of exercise help fight obesity and diabetes. They can also lower the risk of heart disease, one of the most common and

Are Carbs No Good?

In recent years, "no-carb" or "low-carb" diets have become very popular. Bookstores are filled with diet books that talk about the "evils" of carbohydrates. Actually, carbohydrates are *not* evil. They are necessary. We need them for energy. If we remove them from our diet, we eliminate a very important energy source. Some carbohydrates do cause people to store fat, however. The key is learning how to choose the right carbohydrates.

low glycemic carbs

high glycemic carbs

When health experts talk about losing weight, they may talk about the glycemic index. This is a numerical system that measures how fast a carbohydrate triggers the body to make insulin. The higher the number, the faster the sugar response. Carbohydrates with a high glycemic index quickly raise the blood sugar level. They give people an immediate surge of energy. But then the body releases more insulin, which brings the sugar level down too quickly. Then the person may feel weak. Eating foods with a low glycemic index releases energy slowly, providing energy throughout the day. On a scale of 100, with 100 being very high, some foods with a high glycemic index include white bread (96), pretzels (81), french fries (75), donuts (74), and soft drinks (70). Some foods with a low glycemic index include pasta (43), tomatoes (38), yogurt (33), skim milk (32), cherries (22), and peanuts (15).

dangerous complications of diabetes. If more help is needed, there are many effective drugs that can be used.

Transplants

Researchers have been working on other promising diabetes treatments. Some patients with type 1 diabetes have received pancreas transplants. Part or all of a healthy pancreas is placed in a patient. People with successful pancreas transplants may not need to take insulin anymore. The problem with getting a transplant, however, is that the body may identify the new pancreas as foreign. The body's immune system will then attack it and destroy the transplanted cells. This

> The problem with getting a pancreas transplant is that the body's immune system may attack and destroy the transplanted cells.

reaction, called rejection, can make the person very sick. Doctors have to give patients antirejection drugs to make sure this does not happen.

In the United States, pancreas transplants are not common. In 2004, only 603 pancreas transplants were performed.[3] Like any surgery, a transplant involves some risk. It is even more dangerous for people with type 1 diabetes, who already have weakened immune systems. The antirejection drugs can have bad side effects, as well. Therefore, pancreas transplants are usually given only to patients who are not responding to insulin treatments. More often, doctors prefer to perform a combination pancreas-kidney transplant for patients who also have kidney problems. (Kidney failure is a common complication of diabetes.) This way they can take care of two problems at once. In 2004, about 880 pancreas-kidney transplants were performed in the United States.[4]

1999 Miss America Nicole Johnson visits the children's ward at Gunderson Lutheran Medical Center in Wisconsin. Johnson, who has diabetes, was on a speaking tour to raise awareness about diabetes.

6

Living with Diabetes

WHEN NICOLE JOHNSON was crowned Miss America 1999, she could not have been happier. Of course, many young women would be ecstatic to win such a title. But for Nicole, it was more than just a pageant. It was a triumph over diabetes. Nicole was diagnosed with type 1 diabetes when she was nineteen years old, just five years earlier. "'Why me?' was a question I asked when I got diabetes, but the question I was most concerned with was 'How?'—how do I live with this illness and continue to pursue my goals? Exercise, proper nutrition, and insulin have allowed me to control my diabetes."[1] Nicole never lost sight of achieving her dreams. She was not going to let diabetes control *her* life.

As she walked down the runway, with the Miss America song playing, nobody realized that Nicole was wearing an insulin pump underneath her dress. The insulin pump was giving her a continual supply of insulin twenty-four hours a day. It helped to keep her blood sugar level normal to avoid complications associated with diabetes. Before the insulin pump, Nicole had to give herself up to five insulin injections every day. With her busy schedule, it was not easy monitoring her blood sugar level and giving herself daily injections. As Miss America, Nicole had to travel as many as 20,000 miles a month. The insulin pump has given her a sense of freedom. Now she can eat, sleep, and exercise whenever she wants. Sometimes Nicole's busy schedule means missing a meal. But she always keeps a snack handy, such as raisins or pretzels, to give her a quick energy boost. (Eating a snack with a high glycemic index is okay for someone who is taking insulin and misses a meal. It helps to keep the blood sugar level from falling too low.)

People with diabetes need to check their blood glucose levels several times a day to see how well their condition is being controlled. This helps to give a better idea of how much insulin is needed.

Since her diagnosis, Nicole has been speaking out for diabetes research and education. In fact, her goal as Miss America was to educate the public about diabetes. She has accomplished a great deal since she won her title. Nicole has raised more than $16 million for diabetes research. She has also spoken at medical conferences, hospitals, and diabetes care centers. She has written an autobiography called *Living with Diabetes* and co-authored two cookbooks for diabetics. She plays an active role in raising diabetes awareness and publicizing the importance of keeping it under control to prevent serious complications.[2]

Monitoring Glucose Levels

Monitoring glucose is an important part of living with diabetes. People with diabetes need to check their blood glucose levels several times a day to see how well their condition is being controlled. This helps to give a better idea of how much insulin is needed. Blood glucose monitors are devices that can measure blood sugar levels in a matter of minutes. Monitoring glucose levels regularly can help people figure out how much insulin they need.

Blood sugar is tested by pricking a finger or earlobe. A drop of blood is then placed into a small portable

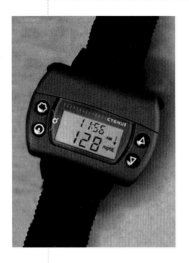

"Ouchless" Monitors?

Many people—especially kids—do not like pricking their fingers several times every day. Researchers have been working on glucose monitors that do not need to prick the skin at all. In August 2002, the Food and Drug Administration approved the GlucoWatch, a glucose-monitoring device for use by children and teenagers with diabetes. (It had been approved for adults in March 2001.) The GlucoWatch is worn on the wrist, like a wristwatch. It uses electricity from a battery to draw fluid through the skin into a pad, where glucose is measured. The watch will give six readings every hour for thirteen hours. If the glucose levels get out of the normal range, an alarm will sound.

The GlucoWatch is still experimental and should not replace fingerstick testing. Although studies have shown that the results are usually close to fingerstick blood glucose tests, the results can vary greatly.

Researchers will continue to work on other painless methods of glucose monitoring. They hope that someday they will develop products that will completely eliminate the need for fingerstick testing.[3]

machine that provides a digital readout of blood sugar levels. People with type 1 diabetes have to test their blood sugar level six times or more every day. Those with type 2 may need to test only once a day or even just once a week.[4] Monitoring blood sugar is very important because it helps the person avoid serious problems that may develop.

Some health experts emphasize "tight control" when they talk about controlling diabetes. *Tight control* means keeping the blood sugar level close to normal as much as possible. This can help prevent complications and can give the person a longer, more active life. A person with good control should have blood sugar levels between 90 and 130 mg/dl before meals. The number should be less than 180 mg/dl two hours after eating a meal. Tight control involves a lot of hard work, though. People on this plan need to pay closer attention to their diet and exercise. Glucose levels also need to be checked more often. Insulin doses need to be adjusted as well. For example, the insulin dose may change according to how much the person plans to eat or how active he or she expects to be. Tight control is not for everyone, but for those who can stick with it, the program can give them more energy and make them feel better.

Insulin Reactions

Getting the right dose of insulin takes some experimenting at first. What may work for one person may not work for another. A health care specialist can help patients come up with a good plan that is just right for that individual.

Sometimes problems may develop if the person misses a dose of insulin or accidentally takes too much. Not enough insulin can result in hyperglycemia, a condition in which the glucose level is higher than normal. Taking too much insulin can result in hypoglycemia, a lower-than-normal glucose level. This can be dangerous. Too much glucose will go out of the blood and will not be carried to the body cells. Remember, the body needs glucose for energy. Without it, the body will not work properly. If the blood glucose level falls too low (below 70 mg/dl) and hypoglycemia develops, insulin shock may result. The person may feel chilly, sweaty, hungry, nervous, and irritable. The person may even faint. Insulin shock is a dangerous condition that needs immediate emergency care.

> If the blood glucose level falls too low (below 70 mg/dl) and hypoglycemia develops, insulin shock may result. Insulin shock is a dangerous condition that needs immediate emergency care.

Sometimes you can get a bad reaction even if you take the right amount of insulin. This might happen if you skip a meal. When you do not eat at the usual time, your blood sugar level goes down. But if you have diabetes and take insulin, you may have already taken your scheduled insulin shot. The insulin was supposed to bring your blood sugar down to normal after a meal. If you do not eat, there will be no extra glucose in your blood. Instead, insulin will take away some of the sugar your body needs.

Exercise burns up glucose, so exercising more than usual can also cause the blood sugar level to fall very low. Eating snacks between meals and before exercising can help avoid an insulin reaction.

Many people with diabetes carry around a quick fix to correct low blood sugar. If they feel dizzy and sick and think they might be getting an insulin reaction, they eat hard candy or take a sweet drink, such as orange juice or soda. The extra sugar goes right into the blood and brings the level back to normal.

Is It Insulin Shock or Diabetic Coma?

An insulin reaction (or insulin shock) is the result of a lower-than-normal sugar level in the blood. A diabetic coma is the result of a higher-than-normal sugar level in the blood. In both conditions the person loses consciousness. How can you tell the difference?

Insulin Shock	Diabetic Coma
Starts suddenly	Develops gradually
Skin pale and moist	Skin dry and hot
Dizziness	No dizziness
Great hunger	Little hunger
Normal thirst	Extreme thirst
Shallow breathing	Deep, difficult breathing
Normal breath odor	Fruity breath odor
Tongue moist	Tongue dry
No vomiting	Vomiting, abdominal pain
Normal urination	Excessive urination
Confusion, strange behavior	Drowsiness, lethargy
Little or no sugar in urine	Large amounts of sugar in urine

Preventing Diabetes

The lifestyle that health experts recommend to help control diabetes can also help prevent the disease. In fact, diet and exercise can even help people with prediabetes to avoid developing diabetes. According to the American Diabetes Association, about thirty minutes of physical activity a day, together with a weight loss of 5 to 10 percent, can reduce a prediabetic person's risk of developing type 2 diabetes by 58 percent.[5] This is the best—and healthiest—way to help keep the blood sugar level under control for people with prediabetes. However, for some people with prediabetes, diet and exercise may not be enough. For them, medications are available that can lower insulin resistance and help bring the blood sugar level back to normal. This can actually help prevent diabetes from developing.

Carry an ID

If you have diabetes, it is a good idea to wear a medical identification bracelet or necklace and carry an ID card in case of an emergency. Make sure it includes your name, the name and number of someone to contact, as well as information about your condition and what to do in case of an insulin reaction. This could save your life.

7

Diabetes and the Future

WILLIAM LACKEY HAS BEEN LIVING with type 1 diabetes and taking insulin since 1949, when he was about five years old. It was not easy being a kid with diabetes. "Immediately I felt different. My brother was two years younger than me and he got all the good stuff in the Easter basket. I got oranges, apples, celery, and carrots and guess what? I stole most of his candy because I didn't get any!"[1]

Over the years, William had trouble keeping his condition under control. Sometimes his usual dose of insulin lowered his blood sugar too much—so low that the glucose meter at the doctor's office could not even get a reading. A number of times he wound up in the hospital because of seizures and blackouts. In fact, he even got into several car accidents when his blood sugar level dropped suddenly. Throughout his life, many doctors have tried to find ways to help William control his diabetes, but nothing worked.

Finally, after searching the Internet, William found out about a pancreas transplant program at the University of Maryland Medical Center. Through e-mails with the acting chief of surgery, Dr. Stephen Bartlett, William found out that he was an acceptable candidate for a pancreas transplant. In January 2001,

"Brittle" Diabetes

Like some other people with type 1 diabetes, William Lackey was what doctors call "brittle." No matter how careful he was about taking his insulin and eating properly, he never could predict what his blood sugar level would be—too high, too low, or just right. People with brittle diabetes often get no warning symptoms when their blood sugar level is dropping, so they do not know they need a quick snack. Suddenly they pass out or have a seizure. For these people, a pancreas or islet cell transplant may be the only hope for a normal life.

William went to the medical center for an evaluation. However, he learned that his insurance company would not cover a pancreas transplant. Then one of the nurses told him about the islet cell transplant program. He was accepted into this program, but he had to wait three years for a donor to become available.

On June 15, 2004, William had the procedure. He spent just four days in the hospital. One month later, William was taking only half as much insulin as he had been. The transplanted islet cells were producing insulin for him. His blood sugar level was staying much closer to normal, and he was no longer having blackouts. "Now I am able to leave the house without fear," he said.[2]

Islet Cell Transplants

Transplants of islet cells are helping a number of people with severe type 1 diabetes. Like William, these people had been unable to keep their blood sugar levels under control with insulin injections or even an insulin pump.

An islet cell transplant involves removing insulin-producing cells (islets) from a donor's pancreas and transferring them into another person. The procedure is not as risky as a pancreas transplant, and it can be performed in less than an hour. The islet cells are transferred to the patient's liver. There they settle down and start producing insulin.

Worldwide, more than 750 islet cell transplants have been performed since the first, in 1974. The early results were disappointing. A year after the transplant, most of the new islet cells had died or had stopped producing insulin. In 2000, however, a group of researchers at the University of Alberta in Edmonton, Canada, dramatically improved the procedure. The Edmonton

Marta Herrera speaks at a press conference after her successful islet cell transplant.

method became the standard for islet cell transplants. Patients are given islet cells from two to four donors, and the antirejection drugs that they take have milder side effects than the ones used in the past. According to a 2004 report, more than half of the eighty-six diabetes patients who received transplants by the Edmonton method no longer needed insulin injections a year after

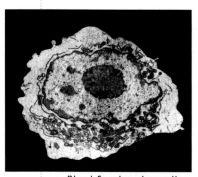

Blood-forming stem cell

Supply and Demand

There are not enough donor pancreases to meet the needs of people with severe type 1 diabetes. Researchers are working on various ways to expand the supply. Stem cells are one possible answer, though there are ethical questions regarding their use. Stem cells are immature cells that have the potential to grow into any kind of cells or tissues in the body. The cells in very early embryos (just a few days after the egg is fertilized) are all stem cells. Even in adults, a tiny fraction of the cells in the bone marrow, liver, spleen, and other tissues are stem cells. Under just the right laboratory conditions, they can be grown into islet cells that produce insulin. Stem cells could provide an unlimited supply of islet cells for transplants.

the final operation. (Usually patients need up to three islet cell transplants to get their blood sugar levels completely under control.)[3]

Harvard researcher Denise Faustman, however, believes that islet cell transplants are not a long-term answer to type 1 diabetes. The immune-system reaction that destroyed the original pancreas will eventually

> Transplants of islet cells are helping a number of people with severe type 1 diabetes. Insulin-producing cells (islets) from a donor's pancreas are transferred to another person.

attack the transplanted islet cells as well. Dr. Faustman believes that the white blood cells that target the islet cells must be killed in order for insulin-producing pancreas cells to survive. In studies on mice, she killed off the white blood cells that cause rejection by injecting a drug called BCG. Then she was going to give her diabetic mice islet-cell transplants. To her surprise, however, the mice started producing insulin on their own. New islet cells were growing in the pancreas. They had apparently developed from stem cells in the spleen.

BCG treatments thus cured diabetic mice. If the same can be done in humans, there would be no need for islet-cell transplants.[4] The Food and Drug Administration has approved the first stage of studies on human patients.[5]

Improving Insulin Treatments

Even if one of the promising lines of diabetes research succeeds, it will take years to develop treatments for widespread use. Meanwhile, insulin is likely to remain an important part of the lives of people with diabetes for some time to come. Researchers are trying to develop new ways of delivering insulin that are more effective and easier to live with. Eliminating the need for injections is a top priority.

There are three main approaches to eliminating insulin shots: inhalers, patches, and pills.[6] Insulin inhalers are the closest to being available. Insulin is breathed in through the mouth and absorbed in the lungs.

Insulin patches can be attached to the skin like a Band-Aid. The patch releases the hormone very slowly. It passes through the skin into the bloodstream. Like an insulin pump, an insulin patch can help keep the blood sugar level stable throughout the day. However, it is much easier to wear and more convenient than the pump. In 2005, insulin patches were in an early stage of testing on humans.

What about pills? People take many medications in the form of pills; why not insulin? The problem is that insulin is a protein, and proteins are digested in the stomach. So insulin taken by mouth would be destroyed before it could get into the bloodstream. Several drug companies are developing insulin pills that can bypass this problem. A jellylike coating protects the insulin from the stomach's acids, and special chemicals carry insulin into the bloodstream.

Researchers are trying to develop new ways of delivering insulin that are more effective and easier to live with. Eliminating the need for injections is a top priority.

Meanwhile, insulin pumps are being improved. Medtronic, a manufacturer of external insulin pumps, has developed an implantable version. The MiniMed 2007 is inserted under the skin of the abdomen and refilled with insulin every two to three months through an implanted tube. The pump delivers insulin in very small amounts directly into the body. A tiny implantable glucose sensor is connected to the pump, and the doses delivered are programmed with a hand-held remote control. Medtronic is working to develop a complete artificial pancreas—an implantable pump that will control the amount of insulin automatically. Its microchip "brain" will set the doses according to the blood glucose levels measured by the implanted sensor.[7]

Researchers at the University of Illinois and Ohio State University have been working on an implantable "insulin pump" that contains real, live insulin-making cells. They are locked inside two-millimeter-long capsules. Food materials from the bloodstream can enter the capsules and insulin can move out into the blood, but antibodies—chemicals that could attack the islet cells—cannot get into the capsules.[8]

New Insights

Doctors have known for a long time that people with diabetes have a high risk of developing heart disease. Just since the early 2000s, however, medical scientists have finally begun to understand why this happens. Several major health problems in today's world are all linked together: obesity, diabetes, and heart disease. The connecting link seems to be inflammation.

Inflammation is a normal body process. You've

probably had a cut or splinter that became infected. You may recall how the skin around it got red, hot, swollen, and very painful. These are the signs of inflammation, which is an important body defense against disease germs.

Usually inflammation is a brief reaction that quiets down as the damage heals. But researchers are discovering that spots of long-term, chronic inflammation may develop. Obesity can play an important role in this. Medical experts now realize, for example, that fat cells are not just storage depots for extra fuel. They are tiny factories that produce hormones and other chemical messengers that affect the whole body. Some of the chemicals that fat cells produce cause inflammation. Others cause blood clots to form inside the blood vessels, and still others cause the blood vessels to narrow and the blood pressure to rise, all of which might lead to a heart attack. One hormone produced by fat cells, called resistin, makes the body cells resistant to insulin.

Researchers at the Joslin Diabetes Center in Boston found that mice fed a high-fat diet became obese, and they also developed insulin resistance. The livers of these mice began to produce increased amounts of a substance linked to inflammation. Then the researchers tinkered with the genes of normal mice to increase their production of the inflammation chemical. These mice soon showed signs of inflammation and insulin resistance. Finally, the researchers treated the mice with aspirin-like drugs. Their inflammation calmed down, and their response to insulin improved. "Insulin resistance seems to be treatable," the researchers reported.[9]

> Researchers now believe that treatment with anti-inflammatory drugs like aspirin may help to control both diabetes and heart disease.

The Joslin experiments were conducted on mice, but there is already some evidence that the same processes are occurring in humans with obesity and type 2 diabetes. For example, heart disease specialists have recently begun using a test for a protein called CRP (C-reactive protein) to diagnose a high risk of heart attacks. CRP is a sign of inflammation. It is also found in people with type 2 diabetes. Researchers now believe that treatment with anti-inflammatory drugs like aspirin

Lizard Spit

The Gila monster is a poisonous lizard found in the southwestern United States. It grows up to two feet long, but it eats just four big meals a year! Between meals it turns its pancreas off, stopping insulin production. When it is ready to eat, a hormone in the Gila monster's saliva turns its pancreas back on and stimulates insulin secretion.

Researchers have created a synthetic form of the Gila monster's hormone, called exenatide, which can also stimulate insulin secretion in humans. It works in the same way as human hormones called incretins, which are produced in the intestines after a meal and stimulate the pancreas. When exenatide was given to patients with type 2 diabetes who had been unable to control their blood sugar level with oral diabetes drugs, they lost weight, and their blood glucose levels fell. New studies now under way are aimed at determining whether exenatide can also benefit people with type 1 diabetes if they still have some working islet cells.[10]

Melvina McCabe

Helping Navajos with Diabetes

Melvina McCabe was born in a hospital next to an American Indian reservation in New Mexico and grew up in the Southwest. In grade school, she dreamed of becoming a doctor. Now she is a family physician and also an associate professor at the medical school of the University of New Mexico. An American Indian herself, she was sad to see the effects of the diabetes epidemic in her community.

Among American Indians in the United States, more than 12 percent of those over the age of nineteen have type 2 diabetes—nearly twice the rate for the general population. The Pima tribe in Arizona has the highest diabetes rate in the world. About 50 percent of all Pima adults between thirty and sixty-four years of age have type 2 diabetes! Diabetes is also increasing among American Indian teenagers. Death rates and complications of diabetes are also much higher among this ethnic group than in the rest of the population.

Some researchers are studying possible genetic links among American Indians and other racial and ethnic groups with high diabetes rates. Meanwhile, Dr. McCabe is focusing on more practical, everyday matters for her Navajo patients. Education on how to manage their condition is very important for all people with diabetes. Dr. McCabe points out, however, that English is a second language for many Navajos, and good translators are a very important part of the care of Navajo patients. The translators need to have some medical knowledge and must know how to explain the disease in words the patients can understand. They must be able to translate the doctors' and nurses' instructions exactly so that the patients know what they have to do to help care for themselves.

In 2000 Dr. McCabe received federal grant money for a five-year study of how Navajo interpreters affect the health of Navajo patients with diabetes. She is comparing a group of patients working with specially trained translators to another group working with Navajo translators who have not received any special training for diabetes work. Another federally sponsored study aims to determine the best teaching methods, comparing classroom instruction with videotapes. Dr. McCabe's own ethnic background has increased her awareness of the challenges facing the American Indian community and inspired her dedication to working to improve their health.[11]

may help to control both diabetes and heart disease. (These would have to be given in carefully determined doses, under a doctor's supervision.)

Searching for Causes . . . and Cures?

Type 1 diabetes develops when the immune system suddenly begins to attack the body's own islet cells, destroying their ability to produce insulin. Researchers believe that discovering just why and how this occurs can lead to ways of stopping and even reversing the damage.

That could lead to a real cure for this form of diabetes, not just ways of controlling and living with the condition.

British researcher Mark Peakman has been working on the problem since the mid-1990s. His research team has discovered chemicals in islet cells that act on certain kinds of white blood cells. Some of these white cells aid in forming antibodies that attack and destroy islet cells. Others calm down inflammation in the islet cells and normally keep the damage under control. Peakman's group has developed a vaccine from some of the islet-cell chemicals. In experiments on mice, the vaccine stopped the destruction of islet cells and promoted the growth of the protective type of white blood cells. The researchers hope that tests on human patients, begun in 2005, will have similar results.[12]

Several other research groups are working on ways to stimulate the growth of insulin-producing cells. American researchers are testing a chemical that stimulates the growth of islet cells in the pancreas and increases the amount of insulin produced in the body. A Japanese research group has discovered ways to stimulate cells in the intestine to produce insulin.

What about type 2 diabetes? Here the islet cells are not the problem. In fact, while type 2 diabetes is developing, the islet cells may even be producing too much insulin—far more than normal—because the hormone is not working properly. What goes wrong here?

Some researchers are focusing on genetic factors, trying to find the genes involved in the development of both obesity and insulin resistance. The science of genetics has made enormous progress in the last few decades. Researchers have now mapped out the full set

The science of genetics has made enormous progress. Researchers have mapped out the full set of genes contained in each human body cell.

of genes contained in each human body cell. They know the chemical structure of these genes and have matched up many of them to their functions in the body. They have also learned how many of these genes produce their effects on the body. "DNA fingerprinting" techniques make it possible to compare the patterns of genes from different people, revealing small differences between individuals. Teams of researchers are now comparing the gene fingerprints of obese people and people with diabetes to those of healthy people. If they can spot particular genes that are found mainly in people with diabetes, and figure out how these genes work, then these genes will be good targets for new drugs to prevent and treat diabetes.

With all the new insights that they are gaining, researchers are making exciting progress toward a cure for diabetes. Meanwhile, modern drugs and devices are allowing people with diabetes to live long and healthy lives.

Questions and Answers

If diabetes is called the sugar disease, does that mean I can get it if I eat too many sweets? No, diabetes is called the sugar disease because the body cannot use sugar properly. It is not caused by eating too many sweets. However, eating too many sweets (or too much of any kind of food) can lead to weight gain, which is a leading risk factor for type 2 diabetes.

Does a person with diabetes have to stay away from sweets? People with diabetes *do* have to watch what they eat. But they don't have to stay away from sweets completely. They just need to choose healthy foods and not eat too many sweets.

My aunt's doctor says she has diabetes, but she's really fat. I thought weight loss was one of the symptoms of diabetes. Weight loss is one of the major symptoms of uncontrolled diabetes. Most type 1 patients are thin, but many people with type 2 diabetes are actually overweight or obese.

What's the difference between type 1 diabetes and type 2 diabetes? In type 1 diabetes, the pancreas makes little or no insulin. Patients have to take insulin injections to keep their blood sugar level normal. In type 2 diabetes, the pancreas may still make insulin, but the body cannot use it properly. Many patients with type 2 diabetes can manage their condition through diet and exercise. Oral medications can also help keep the blood sugar level normal. If diet, exercise, and pills do not work, type 2 patients may need to take insulin injections also.

I just found out that I have type 1 diabetes. Does that mean I have to quit the team? No. There are athletes who have diabetes. They are able to stay active in sports by keeping a daily routine: blood glucose monitoring, regular insulin injections, exercise, and proper nutrition.

I have type 2 diabetes. My doctor says that I am twenty pounds overweight. He told me to lose weight. How come he didn't prescribe insulin shots? A program of diet and exercise will not only help you lose weight, it may also bring your blood sugar level back to normal. Your pancreas is probably still making insulin. It may be able to do its job properly after you lose the excess weight.

I've been taking medication for my type 2 diabetes, and now my lab tests are all normal. Am I cured? Can I stop taking the drugs? There is no cure for diabetes yet. Your doctor may say you can cut back or even stop taking the oral diabetes drugs if you follow a very strict diet and exercise program. But you have to keep it up. If you slack off, your symptoms could come back. Also, you should continue to see your doctor regularly.

Diabetes Timeline

1500 B.C.   Ebers Papyrus of Egypt mentions treatment for diabetes.

400 B.C.   Indian doctor Susruta writes that people with this disease produce "honey urine."

A.D. 100   Greek physician Aretaeus of Cappadocia gives diabetes its name.

1674   English physician Thomas Willis finds out that the urine of people with diabetes is sweet by tasting it himself.

1776   English physician Matthew Dobson proves that sugar is present in the urine of people with diabetes.

1788   English physician Thomas Cawley suggests a link between diabetes and the pancreas.

1790   German physician Johann Peter Frank develops the first diagnostic test for diabetes.

1797   British physician John Rollo discovers that too much sugar in the blood causes excessive urination.

1869   German biologist Paul Langerhans discovers islets of Langerhans in the pancreas.

1889	Joseph von Mering and Oskar Minkowski produce diabetes in dogs.
1921	Frederick Banting and Charles Best of Canada isolate insulin. Nicolae Paulescu does the same in Romania.
1966	The first pancreas transplant is performed.
1979	The world's first pancreas transplant taken from a living donor is performed.
1983	Genetically engineered human insulin becomes available for diabetics.
1992	First gene involved with diabetes is found.
2000	The Edmonton Protocol becomes standard for islet cell transplants.
2002	Researchers begin to link inflammation with insulin resistance and type 2 diabetes.
2005	USFDA approves exenatide injections to treat type 2 diabetes. Insulin inhalers and insulin patches are tested on humans.

For More Information

American Diabetes Association
1701 Beauregard Street
Alexandria, VA 22311
(800) 342–2383
<http://www.diabetes.org>

Canadian Diabetes Association
15 Toronto Street, Suite 800
Toronto ON M5C 2E3
(800) BANTING
<http://www.diabetics.ca/>
<http://www.diabetes123.com/d_0b_250.htm>

Centers for Disease Control and Prevention
Division of Diabetes Translation
P.O. Box 8728
Silver Spring, MD 20910
(877) CDC-DIAB (877-232-3422)
<http://www.cdc.gov/diabetes>

The Dudley Foundation
515 NW Saltzman Rd. #789
Portland, OR 97229
(503) 626-4007
<http://www.chrisdudley.org>

Juvenile Diabetes Research Foundation
International
120 Wall Street
New York, NY 10005-4001
(800) 533-CURE (533-2873)
<http://www.jdrf.org>

National Diabetes Information Clearinghouse (NDIC)
1 Information Way
Bethesda, MD 20892-3560
(800) 860-8747
<http://diabetes.niddk.nih.gov/>

Chapter Notes

Chapter 1. The Sugar Disease

1. The Whittier Institute for Diabetes, "You Can Do Anything," *The Whittier Diabetes Report*, Summer 2002, p. 2, <http://www.whittier.org/pdf/02_Sum.pdf> (December 14, 2004).

2. Rick Philbin, "Interview With Chris Dudley," *Diabetes 123*, November 2004, <http://www.diabetes123.com/sports/ChrisDudley.htm> (December 14, 2004).

3. The Dudley Foundation, "Portland Trail Blazer Chris Dudley Retires," *The Dudley Foundation Supporting Kids With Diabetes*, © 2002–2003, <http://www.chrisdudley.org/> (December 14, 2004).

4. Daniel Trecroci, "Diabetes Didn't Interfere With Dudley's Dream," *Diabetes Health Magazine*, June 1999, <http://www.diabeteshealth.com/read,1038,1515.html> (December 14, 2004).

5. "List of Celebrities With Diabetes," *Information from Answers.com*, *Wikipedia*, <http://www.answers.com/topic/list-of-celebrities-with-diabetes> (April 26, 2005).

6. International Diabetes Federation, "Diabetes Prevalence," *Facts and Figures*, © 2003, <http://www.idf.org/home/index.cfm?node=264> (December 14, 2004).

7. American Diabetes Association, "All About Diabetes," *Diabetes Information*, <http://www.diabetes.org/about-diabetes.jsp> (November 26, 2004).

8. MSNBC News, "Diabetes Now Kills More People Than AIDS," May 5, 2004, <http://www.msnbc.msn.com/id/4907773/> (December 14, 2004).

Chapter 2. Diabetes Through the Ages

1. C. Savona-Ventura, "The History of Diabetes Mellitus: A Maltese Perspective," Diabetic Pregnancy Joint Clinic, Karin Grech Hospital, Malta, 2002, pp. 4–5, <http://www.health.gov.mt/dpjc/history.pdf> (April 29, 2005).

2. "Banting and Best Isolate Insulin 1922," *A Science Odyssey: People and Discoveries*, © 1998, <http://www.pbs.org/wgbh/aso/databank/entries/dm22in.html> (December 22, 2004); "Frederick Banting," *CBC.ca—The Greatest Canadian—Top Ten Greatest Canadians*, © 2004, <http://www.cbc.ca/greatest/top_ten/nominee/banting-frederick.html> (December 22, 2004).

Chapter 3. What Is Diabetes?

1. Marc Bollinger, "Marc Bollinger's Diabetes Story," *Ashley's Diabetes Information Center*, modified September 7, 2004 <http://www.elviradarknight.com/diabetes/marc.html> (December 29, 2004).

2. Daniela Cihakova, "Type 1 Diabetes Mellitus," Johns Hopkins Autoimmune Disease Research Center, September 10, 2001, <http://autoimmune.pathology.jhmi.edu/diseases.cfm?systemID=3&DiseaseID=23> (April 26, 2005).

3. Centers for Disease Control and Prevention, "National Diabetes Fact Sheet," *CDC's Diabetes Program—Publications & Products*, reviewed January 18, 2005, <http://www.cdc.gov/diabetes/pubs/general.htm> (April 29, 2005).

4. Ibid.

5. American Heart Association, "Insulin Resistance," *About Diabetes*, © 2004, <http://www.s2mw.com/heartofdiabetes/resistance.html> (April 29, 2005).

6. Centers for Disease Control and Prevention.

7. American Heart Association.

Chapter 4. What Causes Diabetes?

1. Adapted from: Christine Gorman, "Why So Many of Us Are Getting Diabetes," *Time*, December 8, 2003, pp. 58–67.

2. Cindy Kranz, "Local Girl on *Time* Cover," *The Cincinnati Enquirer*, December 6, 2003, <http://www.enquirer.com/editions/2003/12/06/loc_timekid06.html> (April 26, 2005).

3. North American Association for the Study of Obesity, "Your Weight and Diabetes," © 2003, <http://www.naaso.org/information/diabetes_obesity.asp> (January 12, 2005).

4. Aaron I. Vinik, "Inflammation: The Root of All Evil in Diabetes and the Dysmetabolic Syndrome," Medscape from WebMD, June 1, 2004, <http://www.medscape.com/viewarticle/496269> (April 26, 2005).

5. Suzanne Rostler, "Experts Fear Type 2 Diabetes Epidemic in U.S. Children," *Reuters Health*, September 8, 2000, <http://www.mercola.com/2000/sep/17/diabetes_epidemic.htm> (January 12, 2005).

6. D. A. Pyke, "The History of Diabetes," Diabetic Department, King's College Hospital, London, UK, © 2000, <http://www.diabetesliving.com/basics/wiley.htm> (December 16, 2004).

7. Gorman.

8. Paula Ford-Martin with Ian Blumer, M.D., *The Everything Diabetes Book*, Avon, Mass.: Adams Media, 2004, p. 16.

9. American Diabetes Association, "National Diabetes Fact Sheet," *All About Diabetes*, <http://www.diabetes.org/diabetes-statistics/national-diabetes-fact-sheet.jsp> (April 26, 2005), adapted from Centers for Disease Control and Prevention, *National Diabetes Fact Sheet: General Information and National Estimates on Diabetes in the United States, 2002*, Atlanta, Ga.: U.S. Department of Health and Human Services, Centers for Disease Control and Prevention, 2003.

Chapter 5. Testing and Treatment

1. David Behrend, "Diabetes Death Stirs a Memory," *The Courier News*, February 28, 1998, pp. A-1, A-4.

2. Ibid.

3. AASLD (The American Association for the Study of Liver Diseases), "Facts About Transplantation," March 11, 2005, <https://www.aasld.org/eweb/DynamicPage.aspx?Site=AASLD3&webcode=facttransplantation> (August 15, 2005).

4. Ibid.

Chapter 6. Living with Diabetes

1. Girlpower.gov, "Meet Miss America 1999, Nicole Johnson," revised January 31, 2005, <http://www.girlpower.gov/girlarea/gpguests/johnson.htm> (August 18, 2005).

2. CBN.com, "Nicole Johnson Baker: Living the 'dLife'," August 3, 2005, <http://www.cbn.com/700club/Guests/Bios/Nicole_Johnson_Baker080305.asp> (August 15, 2005).

3. U.S. Food and Drug Administration, "FDA Approves GlucoWatch Device for Children with Diabetes," press release, August 27, 2002, <http://www.fda.gov/bbs/topics/NEWS/2002/NEW00830.html> (January 25, 2005).

4. American Diabetes Association, "Tight Diabetes Control," December 9, 2004, <http://www.diabetes.org/type-1-diabetes/tight-control.jsp> (April 27, 2005).

5. American Diabetes Association, "How to Prevent or Delay Diabetes," *Diabetes Prevention*, December 22, 2004, <http://www.diabetes.org/diabetes-prevention/how-to-prevent-diabetes.jsp> (April 28, 2005).

Chapter 7. Diabetes and the Future

1. William Lackey, "55-Year Diabetic 'Can Now Leave the House Without Fear' After Islet Cell Transplant," *University of Maryland Medical Center: Islet Cell Patient Testimonial*, July 19, 2004, <http://www.umm.edu/transplant/isletcell_transplant.html> (January 28, 2005).

2. Ibid.

3. Joan Chamberlain, "Centers Report Islet Transplant Results in Patients With Type I Diabetes," NIH News, September 7, 2004, <http://www.nih.gov/news/pr/sep2004/niddk-07.htm> (January 28, 2005).

4. Gina Kolata, "I Beg to Differ: A Diabetes Researcher Forges Her Own Path to a Cure," *New York Times*, November 9, 2004, p. F-6.

5. JoinLeeNow Faq, "The Iacocca Foundation and JoinLeeNow," December 2004, <http://www.joinleenow.org/html/press/pdf/faq_a.pdf> (August 18, 2005).

6. Terri Kordella, "The Future of Insulin," *Diabetes Forecast*, March 2003, <http://www.diabetes.org/diabetes-forecast/mar2003/future.jsp> (January 27, 2005).

7. "Implantable Insulin Pump Closer to Becoming a Reality," *Defeat Diabetes*, July 18, 2002, <http://www.defeatdiabetes.org/Articles/pump020718.htm> (February 3, 2005).

8. "Implantable Insulin Pumps," *LifeClinic*, © 2002, <http://www.lifeclinic.com/focus/diabetes/advances.asp> (January 26, 2005).

9. Miranda Hitti, "Aspirin-Like Drugs May Fight Type 2 Diabetes," *WebMD Medical News*, February 1, 2005, <http://my.webmd.com/content/Article/100/105527.htm> (February 3, 2005).

10. American Diabetes Association, "What Do a Vampire Bat and a Gila Monster Have in Common?" *Forefront*, Winter/Spring 2005, pp. 20–21.

11. Melvina L. McCabe, MD, "Improving Diabetes Translations in the Navajo Language—a Pilot Study," *Forefront*, Summer/Fall 2004, pp. 11–13.

12. Rob Saunders, "A New Dawn for Prevention?" *Diabetes Update*, Spring 2005, pp. 22–25.

Glossary

amputation—The surgical removal of all or part of a limb or digit (finger or toe).

antibodies—Large proteins produced by white blood cells that recognize and attack "foreign" chemicals, including those on the outer surface of bacteria, cells that have been infected by viruses, and cancer cells. The immune system may mistakenly label certain normal body cells (such as insulin-producing beta cells) as "foreign" and produce antibodies against them.

autoimmune reaction—A mistaken attack by the immune system on the body's own cells.

autopsy—The examination of a body after death to determine the cause of death and to locate evidence of disease or injury.

beta cells—Cells in the islets of Langerhans in the pancreas that release the hormone insulin.

blood sugar level—The amount of glucose in the blood.

carbohydrates—Starches and sugars, the body's main energy sources.

cholesterol—A fatty substance produced in the body and found in plaque that clogs arteries.

C-reactive protein (CRP)—A blood protein that is found in higher than normal amounts when inflammation is present in the body.

diabetes insipidus—A rare type of diabetes in which large amounts of urine are produced, but the urine does not contain sugar.

diabetes mellitus—A condition in which insulin is not produced or does not properly control the body's use and storage of sugar, resulting in abnormally high amounts of glucose in the blood; extra glucose may also pass out of the blood and be excreted in the urine.

diabetic coma—A serious condition caused by a lack of insulin, resulting in a buildup of ketones from using fats for energy. Headache, tiredness, stomach pains, and a loss of consciousness may occur just before coma.

fasting plasma glucose test—A diagnostic test in which the blood glucose level is measured early in the morning, before eating.

genes—Chemicals inside each cell that carry inherited traits.

gestational diabetes—A type of diabetes that appears in some women during pregnancy, then disappears after the baby is born.

glucagon—A hormone that causes the release of stored glucose from the liver and raises the blood sugar level.

glucose—The most common kind of sugar in the blood. The body uses glucose for energy.

glucose tolerance test—A test for diabetes in which a person drinks a glucose solution after fasting and the blood sugar is measured several times over the next three hours.

glycemic index—A numerical system that measures how fast a carbohydrate triggers the body to make insulin.

hormone—Any of the chemicals that help control the body's activities.

hyperglycemia—A higher-than-normal blood sugar level.

hypertension—High blood pressure.

hypoglycemia—A lower-than-normal blood sugar level.

inflammation—Redness, heat, and swelling that develop when tissues are damaged.

inherited—Passed on by genes from parents to children.

insulin—A hormone that lowers the amount of sugar in the blood and increases the storage of sugar in the liver.

insulin reaction (insulin shock)—Hypoglycemia resulting from taking too much insulin (or failing to eat the expected amount of food after taking insulin).

Dizziness, confusion, and unconsciousness may develop as the blood sugar level falls.

insulin resistance—A condition in which the cells are unable to use insulin effectively.

islets (*pronounced* EYE-lets)—Clusters of hormone-producing cells scattered through the pancreas; also called islets of Langerhans. They include beta cells, which produce insulin.

ketoacidosis—A buildup of toxic ketones in the blood that occurs when the body is using fats instead of sugars as energy fuel.

ketones—Chemicals with a fruity odor that are formed when the body burns fats for energy.

mutate—To change in form.

obesity—The condition of being extremely overweight.

pancreas—An organ that produces hormones, such as insulin and glucagon, that help to control the amount of glucose in the blood; it also makes digestive juices, which help to break down food.

plasma glucose test—A diagnostic test in which the blood sugar level is measured; it can be taken at any time of the day.

prediabetes—A condition of higher-than-normal blood sugar level (between 100 and 125 mg/dl), but not yet diabetes; it increases the risk for developing type 2 diabetes.

rejection—Attack by the immune system on transplanted cells or organs.

starch—A food substance found in bread, potatoes, and pasta that the body breaks down into sugars.

stem cells—Immature cells that have the potential for developing into any type of cell or tissue.

Further Reading

Betschart-Roemer, Jean. *Type 2 Diabetes in Teens: Secrets for Success*. New York: John Wiley & Sons, 2002.

Gray, Shirley Wimbish. *Living with Diabetes*. Chanhassen, Minn.: Child's World, 2003.

Hyde, Margaret O., and Elizabeth H. Forsyth. *Diabetes*. New York: Franklin Watts, 2003.

Petit, Willam A., Jr., and Christine Adamec. *The Encyclopedia of Diabetes*. New York: Facts on File, 2002.

Rubin, Alan L. *Diabetes for Dummies*. New York: Wiley Publishing, Inc., 2001.

Internet Address

(See also **For More Information**, p. 109)

Diabetes 123.com, Inc. *Children with Diabetes.* © 1995–2005. <http://www.childrenwithdiabetes. com/index_cwd.htm>.

Juvenile Diabetes Research Foundation International. *Kids Online.* © 2004. <http://kids.jdrf.org>.

National Institutes of Health and the Centers for Disease Control and Prevention. *National Diabetes Education Program.* <http://www.ndep.nih.gov>.

Index

pancreas transplant, 31–32, 74–75, 87
Peakman, Mark, 100
penlet device, **63**
Pima Indians, 56, 98
plasma glucose test, 62
Pope John Paul II, 14
prediabetes, 43, 58, 63, 85
pregnancy, 44, 58
Presley, Elvis, 14

R

resistin, 95
Robinson, Jackie, 14
Rollo, John, 20
rubella virus, 57

S

seizure, 87
siphon, 18
sports, 12, 65
starch, 10, 20, 39, 40
statistics, 15, 41, 43, 53, 54, 56, 58, 98
stem cells, 90
Stone, Sharon, 14
stroke, 48
sugar, 20, 24, 37, 38, 40, **46**, 47
sugar in urine, 19–20, 21, 38, 47, 84
Susruta, 17–18

T

Taylor, Elizabeth, 14
television, **55**
Thompson, Leonard, 27, **28**
tight control, 81
transplant, 74–75
transplant rejection, 32, 74
twins, 56
type 1 diabetes, 40–41, 47, 74, 77, 99
    risk factors, 57
type 2 diabetes, 42, 47, 51, 56, 70, 96, 97, 100
    risk factors, 53, 55, 57–58

U

uncontrolled diabetes, 47, 48
urine, 37, 38, 45, **46**, 47
urine tests, 62

V

vaccine, 100
viruses, 57
von Mering, Joseph, 22

W

weight loss, 42, 44, 62
Wells, H. G., 14
white blood cells, 41, 91, 100
Williams, Vanessa, 14
Willis, Thomas, 19